Praise

"Like Bukowski and other great American poets who lived
their words, Phill Provance mines his soul to bring light to
the dark places of life ... and tell a tough story with a hint of
humor and horror."
JOHN MCCAFFREY, THE GOOD MEN PROJECT

"Ingenious ... I feel like I'm looking into a diorama in a
shoebox, a scene and a world dreamily composed within the
cleanly-wrought borders of the speaker's imagination ... a
little myth with a Midwestern twang."
DIANE SEUSS, 2016 PULITZER PRIZE FINALIST

"The lure of the archaic is a notional time travel in which
supposed Denton Morrises may enjoy games of fancy dress and
do the voices in decades more forgiving to chiming rhymes.
Its comedy arrives in the form of a seriousness of technical achievement belied by a sometime silliness of content.
How does one take such poems? I take them as utopian, as
belonging, almost politically, to a never-appearing age of poetry
that is as permissive as it is beholden to the past. In this
unusual poetry of strangely familiar sounds, one discovers a
space for rarely seen lyric promises as oddly compacted as they
are true."
CHRIS HOSEA, 2013 WALT WHITMAN AWARD WINNER

"I was glad to be introduced to Phill Provance's poetry,
which sets itself apart from ordinary competence through
qualities of acute intelligence and technical skill. He knows
that a poem is a lens on experience and that the best way to
represent the multifaceted thing we call reality is to apply to
it as many and diverse lenses as you can manage. Here is a
book that deserves a cordial welcome."
ALFRED CORN, 1982 LEVINSON PRIZE WINNER, ACADEMY OF
AMERICAN POETS, NEA AND GUGGENHEIM FELLOW

"It would be tempting to compartmentalize *A Plan in Case of Morning* in terms of its three sections, 'Going Out,' 'Going Under,' and 'Coming In,' but this collection of poems is equally charged throughout, just as dynamic in its last poem as in its first, and rich with form, from the prose poems 'How It Goes' and 'The Stenographers Union' to 'Elegy for My College Roommate,' with its carefully crafted measures of white space. *A Plan in Case of Morning* is a coming-of-middle-age chronicle of sorts, and it is against this backdrop that we find lines such as those in 'Gen Y Love Poem': 'which is to say/I am still in it/for myself/to keep you there/is still the mystery/ of whether I will/stay.' Moreover, Provance visits with the interior in a way as dynamic as it is delicious and powerful, as in 'My Old Man,' where we find the lines 'In three months I'll come home to find him/planted on his couch, the upholstery full/of burn holes, him sucking on tin foil/ "getting the good cocaine out," the desk/clutter in some corner,' while poems like 'Now' leave a delicious bruise, with the lines 'And it occurs I've wasted/my best words on one/who didn't deserve/a pronoun.' Provance writes, in 'A New Kind of Vegan,' 'I want to watch you eat my words. Sprinkle/some salt on them. Serve them/on a bed of lettuce skins.' Any reader of *A Plan in Case of Morning* will be happy to devour."
JACINDA TOWNSEND, WINNER OF THE 2015 JAMES FENIMORE COOPER AND JANET HEIDINGER KAFKA PRIZES

About the Author

Phill Provance was born in Mt. Pleasant, Pennsylvania, an Appalachian valley town of roughly 5,000 people, to a Kirby salesman and a welfare caseworker who divorced when he was four. Subsequently spending his early years in a trailer on his grandparents' farm, he witnessed the same alcoholism, drug abuse, mental illness, domestic violence, and poverty that figure into most stereotypes of Appalachia. Nevertheless, with his parents' unconditional love and the example of his mother—who eventually completed her PhD. in Plant Biology—Phill excelled as a student, winning his first scholastic writing prize at age six and simultaneously studying French, German and Latin in junior high and high school.

Since leaving home at eighteen, he's published comics, nonfiction, journalism, and poetry in numerous newspapers, journals, and magazines throughout the English-speaking world. Meanwhile, he's completed his bachelor's degree in English Literature and German Language at Bethany College and Oxford University and received his MFA in both Poetry and Fiction from WV Wesleyan College. *A Plan in Case of Morning* (Vine Leaves Press, Sept. 2020), is his third book. His other works include the nonfiction popular history *A Brief History of Woodbridge, New Jersey* (The History Press 2019) and the poetry chapbook *The Day the Sun Rolled Out of the Sky* (Cy Gist Press 2010). Currently a resident of the Chicago area, he is a graduate student in the University of Illinois at Chicago's highly selective Program for Writers. His second full-length work of nonfiction, *Postcards of McHenry County, Illinois*, is forthcoming from Arcadia Publishing.

phillprovance.com

A Plan
in Case of
Morning

Phill Provance

Vine Leaves Press
Melbourne, Vic, Australia

Print Edition
ISBN: 978-1-925965-40-7
Published by Vine Leaves Press 2020
Melbourne, Victoria, Australia

Cover design by Jessica Bell
Interior design by Amie McCracken

A catalogue record for this book is available from the National Library of Australia

For all our future spacemen,
but especially for Ledger

Table of Contents

What woman wants a fireman,
a plan in case of morning,
a man with hands like Hoover Dams
who makes an easy hundred grand,
who trades his Viper for a van,
a man who's, frankly, boring?

I

Going Out

Nowhere was his home,
But swiftly he went his way.
Many a lonesome road he roamed—
Or so the books about him say.

– Sir Gawayn and þe Grene Knyȝt

Chicago Tableau

For D. Revell

It started with an umbrella.
Striped pink and green with
a mangled frame, ribs missing,
shaft bent, it lay on a piano
beside a top and yo-yo.

It started as a man dressed
in pinstriped pants, white shirt,
red bowtie and suspenders
frowned, his mussed, blond bangs
matted to his forehead.

It started with a woman,
the fine curls on the back of her neck
as it craned over the keyboard
and her slender hands poised over
the keys, as if debating
which to depress.

It started with the piano's
walnut sheen—and a vase with
crisp irises, the yo-yo and blouse
and a stiff, gray cat by the pedals
all seemed to gasp in unison.

But it started like this
and ended like this.
For then there was a flash of white light

at the crosswalk, and a flood
of feet and arms washed down
Wabash, bowling me away,
and still, to this hour, I have no clue
what those mannequins were doing.

Gen Y Love Poem

When I text you,
Platonic kissy face, rest
assured I do not
mean, *I love you,* so much
as I love the halfhearted
ironic gesture, rest
assured I am still

lean-faced as any
dust devil, still
willing to devour
you, still ready to
drag you up
a long flight
of Chicago high
-rise steps, club or
cocktail in hand,
rest
assured I still mean
I love listening to you
talk of Tartars and
Saladin and how
Mehmed II compares
favorably with
Erdogan. Trust me,
my love
is still trying
to glimpse
the titles of others'
books around wrought
-iron chairs and sunny
dry-eyed Ficuses
on any veranda
under any tricolor
awning in Wicker Park
with you—

which is to say
I am still in it
for myself,
to keep you there
is still the mystery
of whether I will
stay.

The Poet as the Sea

[At the Kursaal by Southend Pier]

How nice would it be to be
the sea when you first take a
dip in spring. Sploshing full of
watery thoughts, I'd feel you

                    plunge in,
then race my current towards the
beach, to rinse you in warm tides,
the whishing seagulls drifting in
in languid, long, low dives.

              Of course,
what modesty exists between
a swimmer and the sea? Amidst
the sunlight's tickling gleam, I
couldn't help myself

           but stream
into your two-piece top and slish
along your belly, hips and thighs
until, at last, I'd splash into
your nostrils, mouth and eyes.

The fattest monk in history

was certifiably Thomas Aquinas,
who at his death weighed so much
he had to be removed from his
monastery with a medieval crane—
which was probably a trebuchet
rigged specifically for this purpose.

My connection to Aquinas is I am a
sodomite—not by nature but because
as a student at a pre-seminary college
I was made to read his treatise defining
sodomy, the delectable outrage of the
Vulgate translated to describe for me,
unassuming 21st century American boy,
what parts ought not one insertibus into anus.

I imagine old Thomas limp and gray
hoisted out over the quadrangle,
one arm beneath his robes, distended
from full-fist insertion, the other
hand clenched around his neck
in a perfect prayer for the Beatitudes.

How It Goes

The woman shoves her way deeper into the forest, thrusting aside some beech limbs blocking her path. I watch her freckled shoulders and thighs disappear behind a thicket of brambles and picture her shimmying into red heels, miniskirt and faux-mink jacket. Then I discover the back of my head has been resting the entire time against a potato-size piece of limestone and is buried up to the ears in a thick tuft of moss.

With nothing else to do, I light a cigarette and look up. The bare, black branches form a net to catch the sky as two black birds jostle in the treetops. Crows, it appears, and whether they are playing or fighting is impossible to tell. All I know is what I see: one bird carries a holly twig in its beak, a single scarlet berry dangling from one end, while the other follows several feet behind, bouncing along the slender bough where they both landed.

Then, gaining on the first crow, the second nips at the berry, and the pair scuffle. Their beaks forget the twig amid flapping and cawing, and it drops to the forest floor, striking my chest berryless. Suddenly, I realize   I   am   cold.

Woman Hips, Woman Lips, Woman Spine

Woman hips, woman lips, woman spine,
where did you slip your magic ship-shine?
Shakes my breath, riddles my chest,
a ghost-limb bullet felt as place where no
place should be, as the hammer clicks time on time.

And, woman hips, woman lips, woman spine,
what fine rose stem rose to make your parts,
fills the toilette bowl with blood the color of
sky before a tornado comes and drums a silt sty
behind the window dressing of my eyes?

What can I or any man do but feel the need
to scream and apologize to you? What can I do
but let you dig your heels into my side,
let your hands rise along my own spine's rusted rise
and jostle the brittle ribs you left behind?

So then, woman heart, woman mind,
sew my lips against the outrage of daylight,
lay the truce between your God and mine,
learn to rope and drag the moon until
settling it all with a spoonful of soup

you make the waters still the tide,
shutter the sill for the Earth's last line.

Soft Monster

Even now I could jab you, tickle you,
your teeth cresting the headboard like
a shark prepared to devour my head.
Even now I could snuggle and kiss you,
pick thin wisps of monster fluff
from the pulp of my lips.

Even as you prepare to grind my ribs,
boil me, frappe my minuscule digits with a
dash of orange juice, I could lash myself
to one gargantuan, smooth leg
and watch the landscape scroll
as we bound together
over the mountains.

Triangle

It doesn't matter—
love, right,
Bermuda—

as Plato reminds us
it exists nowhere
but in thought.

But how graceful
its stark, black lines
traced with a ruler

on flat-white paper,
how nice to see
the contrast

tidy, defined
sharp as a pair
of pruning shears.

And how the numbers'
buzzy infinity
breaks against its sine

its tangent, radials and pi,
unknowable inside
unknowable

as God
become a slice
by which coordinates

and degree combine
into a trinket box
with an edge

as sheer as night.

A New Kind of Vegan

I want to watch you eat my words. Sprinkle
some salt on them. Serve them
on a bed of lettuce skins.
          *
Lettuce is mostly water. Water is
mostly air. Most things are
mostly this way.
          *
When a lettuce is chopped, a little
air squeezes out. This is what
passes for a death rattle.
          *
Most of my words are
a kind of salt. I am
mostly a lettuce.

Magdalen College

As much as you think
you'd see its branches drooping,
the Plane's leaves all glow green
as a stray bobby twirls his truncheon
while passing the wrought-iron gate,

as the college's ketton face throws orange cascades
into the road's murky potholes
and the sky, bleared with only faint streaks of gray,
has been punctured by sunlight
warming you in your Macintosh
till sweat prickles your calves in your galoshes.

It's just another day, says the breeze,
and the spiral of rooks above the tower
seems to echo this awful pronouncement:
the rest of the world will go
on and on and on

in its monotonous monotone drone
as if you have lost nothing,
as if the last plash from the last lorry to pass
has already evaporated
from your coat.

What I Said to Her Was Not a Lie

> *"As the honeysuckle vine and the hazel entwine*
> *so did the queen and her Tristan survive,*
> *for only together was either alive*
> *and where they were parted a part of them died."*

> – *Marie de France, "Chevrefoil"*

I was in love with a girl once
and told her there was a sacred
part of the night for her.
I said it wasn't the dinner part
or the sex part or the sleeping part;

it was the part when we both
lay in the marigold lamplight,
feeling like how the desert must feel
when the wind slides its hand across it.
I said, if I were a light bulb and she
were a lampshade, then at those times
I would turn inside out
and shine outside in.

Now there is no girl.

Well, there are many—
which is just as well.

I do not say, *There is a sacred part*
of the night for you, to anyone.

Sometimes I lie in bed
and trace her face
on the ceiling and walls
until my eyes feel like
two busted light bulbs.

I know that she is
somewhere else

and that someone else is
saying those things to her.
I hope he doesn't say
them quite so well
or that I continue
to say them best.

II

Going Under

Halfway down the path of life
I got lost in a darkened wood,
For I'd forgot which way was right.

– Dante Alleghieri, Inferno

Between You and Me

Now let's examine how pathos works:
I'll proffer my dirt; I'll
tell you about the beautiful olive
-colored boogers I used to hide
beneath my parents' couch when
I was five
          or how, when
I walk into the office mornings,
I take a sip from a fresh bottle of the
carbonated water the company provides,
remember it gives me dry mouth
and place the rest in the refrigerator.

I would say, *Do not be alarmed,*

but of course you won't. You will think,
I did that too, except
I put my boogers
beneath the radiator.

Los Dos Joaquines

"Will your transformation: oh get lost in the flame!
For therein lies desire, flaunting an ever-elusive change."

– *Rainer Maria Rilke,* Die Sonette an Orpheus

When we are old, my friend, will we remember
our nights in Grand Central's gilt-framed halls
and beautiful blonde women sucking on clam shells
and beautiful brunettes with black-marble thighs?

And will we recall those taut-noose Fridays
stuffed in some crevice of a cocktail lounge,
scraping the week out with Potter's martinis
and slipping the waitresses left-over ice?

Will we remember each vagabond sunrise,
drinking our breakfasts in Paddy Byrne's pub,
troubadour strumming beneath Barnard's windows
and guitar string-cut fingers and still-lost loves?

Or will we, like the old men now crowding the Arch,
sit church-eyed behind our wire-brush beards
and, sighing through sets of tobacco-tanned lips,
try to castle our rooks with our pawns?

Snapchat Triolet

They finally tore down the house on West Church
where all the kids used to get stoned and get plastered.
After the sheriff performed a tax search,

they finally tore down the house. On West Church
all you see by the overgrown birch
are scaly tar shingles on one rotted rafter.

Now that they've torn down the house on West Church
where do we go to get stoned and get plastered?

Now

in a bar, staring
at the bister liquids
martially arrayed in stiff-necked
bottles, my glasses and cap are off
in an attempt to look younger
when the truth is
I'm just some
nondescript
stranger,
some old creep
shooting for hip.
And it occurs I've wasted
my best words on one
who didn't deserve
a pronoun.
Of course, I tried.
Bought us a house,
mid-American Taj Mahal
decked to the rafters in leather furniture,
carpet with pile so high you'd swear you'd drown,
a brand-new dishwasher, Keurig, flat screens,
steel-tone linings, everything black or gray,
with which I prayed to corral my loss.
Still, I dutifully continue to pay
the mortgage, have learned
a woman to start with
must be mad
to want a poet
for a man. So now
I wake mornings to cruel quiet,
drink the last stale backwash
and stare at my toiletries
in their tiny phalanx.
And tomorrow
or someday
after you
will find
a lump

at the end of the bar.
That'll be me:
too young
to think,
too old
to live
on fables.

Too Funny

After Jean Follain

Drunk one morning
beneath the sallow night,
the teacher fell asleep
on a massage bed at his gym.
The warm jets of water
nuzzling his muscles
and prying at his bones
with delicate fingers,
he slept there three hours
without a soul to wake him,
then drove home soberly
fleeing a migraine.

His story now finished,
the blonde waitress frowns
at tumblers and jiggers
arrayed like small houses
while, huddled adjacent,
his painter friend howls
till tears swarm his eyes
like skylarks.

Outside Odessa

Such is not presaged: passage pressed
between limp barns and nodding wheat,
barbwire slicing a weary tangent
past oak and Osage trees.

      The clock
in the dashboard fizzles in agreement
with the sun, which leans its strained eye
on a nearby silo. And I take all this to mean time
has collapsed to the space of a stop sign.

A blackbird sits on a telephone line, and I ask him,
Where are we?
     Odessa, he says.
        Where's that?
But his interest has left. Picking a tick from his down
he turns away: *Likely as day, you fell off your perch.*

It's hard to argue with a blackbird's sense.
Mussed as the crowns of wheat I begin to walk.
Naturally, whatever was bound to be is now not.

The Stenographers Union

Darko, why can't you sleep? Right now the Stenographers Union is inflating the moon just over that hill. Soon, the moon will catch fire in the back room of a Halloween-novelty shop. The S.U. is already dissecting Crawford Avenue brick by brick. The moon is just a jellyfish we all have a spoon in.

Darko, your eyes are falling out. The Grand Stenographer is loading his standard-issue pocket protector. Eventually, he will don the wig of a 70-year-old German janitor. Eventually, each of his teeth will become a perfect scale replica of Nebraska.

Then, old Monsignor Le G.S. will look a bit more like you and me—you, who aren't as serious as we might sound—*you* with your heart like a toothless rattle! But aren't we the generation of hard luck and broken parts; don't our iron crosses just float as well as witches.

When the last one left

a knife lay on
the kitchen table for
three days.

It was an eight-inch
chef's knife
she'd been slicing

a Christmas orange with.
Now, I'm normally
a tidy man, but you see,

she left the day the sun
rolled out of the sky
demanding to know

who had stolen his shoes.
He beamed darkly at
the chief of police and refused

to leave the place
where the World War II
monument had stood.

So it was three days
of trying to spray
him out with fire hoses,

while the children bathed
and roasted marshmallows
from the roof of Town Hall.

Then, on the third day,
the moon alighted
and admitted

to stealing the sun's
shoes. So I went home
to find the knife

and a seed fused to
the caramelized juice.
And I decided right then

that I'd never let
another woman
cut a Christmas orange.

Hard to Say

The sky is miserable. It was going to have
its own little tea party, but no one came.
Such a pity too: the new tea pot gave off
such a brilliant sheen, and the spoons
reflected so flawlessly.
But, to top it off, it is that time
of the month for the sky. It feels
like a precisely written note
in which each letter has been drawn
exactly the size of a sand flea—so precisely,
in fact, that packed in each letter is a tiny box
and in each box is an even smaller letter
the size of a sea monkey. Yes, let's think
of sea monkeys. They are so nice
and enter cryptobiosis so civilly
that shipping their eggs seems no work at all.
What is *cryptobiosis*?
I assume it's like *cryptofascist*
but with borax and yeast. We are all
so tiny in our own tiny lives
that it's hard to say
anything.

St. Petersburg Has Many Churches

St. Petersburg has many churches that no one prays in.
Their soft serve-swirl spires are ironic like that.
You and I ellipticizing the Savior on the Spilled Blood,
speaking of what to name our housecat
as we drag our fingers along the garden's toy gates and walls—
that is also ironic.

If there is anything ironic about St. Petersburg
it's that no one may hold its soft spires.
Or wouldn't there be spilled blood and a toy cat praying in the gardens?
Or you and I ellipticizing our house name,
wouldn't that also be a church?

When you look at a tree in a garden
it is clearer if you look at all the things that are not a tree.
When you sleep under a blanket
it is important to remember it's not the blanket that is warm
but the space between it and your skin.

I heard it is day for so long in St. Petersburg
that you forget that blankets are warm.
I also heard it's so cold that when you piss
the stream freezes into a yellow arch.
The first statement is true;
the second is ironic.

The cat and I think speaking of you in a house makes a gate ironic.
How else to explain the many names of spilled gardens?
If I had to forget about the day in warm blankets
I would do it by ellipticizing trees no one prays in.
I would drag my fingers in the toy blood on the walls
and piss on the church spires.

Why the Coyote Doesn't
Just Order Chinese

No money. That Coyote's a survivalist. He converted all his currency into precious metals and Swiss Army knives back in '08. The setting is obviously New Jersey. Obviously, the bomb has already dropped. Obviously, the laws of physics no longer apply. The Coyote, in fact, is not a Coyote but a man, and all the Acme shit and the Road Runner himself are just figments of his imagination. Really, his name is Bob. He's the lone survivor of a nuclear war. He whips his body wildly at an imagined bird, imagining himself an equally small canine. It's ridiculous, he knows. But what else is there to do when you are a meter underground and the last of your kind? You might as well dream big or go home.

So he dreams of explosions. He dreams of contraptions. He dreams in technicolor, deep in his underground bunker. He's about 70 or so—maybe 80 max. His hundred-thousand C-Rations and cans of peas have long since been opened and their contents devoured alone so that their containers litter his safe cave like so many empty bombshells. Two weeks ago, he ate the last tin of Viennese Wieners, the very last food left after 40 years. Now, he is starving—listen:

That is the sound of him starving. But in his dreams, he's getting closer. Each dream he thinks of falling off a cliff. He is getting there, and each time it happens, he arises perfect, whole, finally unscathed, ready to assemble the cogs, gears and pulleys that are the next mechanism of tomorrow.

Counter-play

I split a match with an ax when I was ten,
drew back and watched the blade glide
through its round, red head, watched it spark
and swallow itself in flame, down to the notch
in the stump it was set in.

                I imagined there must
be a boy in some opposite place, with another stump
and another ax raised over his shoulders and that,
after my flame had burrowed into the wood, it had
scaled another thin, pine shaft and collapsed into
another polished match head.

Then I heard not-me not-strike his not-stump,
and his flame fizzled into my next match.
So I stood back and lifted my ax again,
let it glide a second time—except now I had
determined to miss.

            And, when my blade
had come down, I watched blood climb,
like a midday moonrise from the new-made slit.

Great Expectations

In 1987 it was hot in Pennsylvania, so hot they cancelled baseball practice and I had to stay home with my grandmother, with nothing to do but watch the ragweed in my mother's garden turn yellow. I started walking out to the end of our gravel driveway twice a day to check the mailbox and to watch for my mother's car. Sometimes I would lie on the hood of grandma's red Chevette and look for elephants and giraffes among the clouds till the searing steel burned the back of my head and neck.

Then, one day as I was digging a divot in the front yard (convinced by Bugs Bunny I could dig my way to China), a broad, black shadow skimmed the grass blades in front of me. I looked up, and there was the belly of a massive bird, its wings broad as I was tall. It glided towards the cornfield and alighted among the toppled, dry stalks, and I saw it there, large, erect, brown-black plumage rippling as its muscles settled, like a divine protector, a sign from God. So I dashed for our gray-sided trailer, shouted, *Grandma, come see, a bald eagle!*

But when her cotton-ball head poked out the doorway, I saw her hips shift, saw her adjust her glasses, and she said, *Fool child. That ain't no eagle, it's a vulture.*

A fulture?

Yeah, a vulture. See it ain't got no white feathers on its head?

But it's bald.

A bald eagle ain't really bald.

Then why do they call it bald?

Because they're more foolish than you.

Then, she slammed the screen door, probably went back to her book or crossword, and I sat staring at the vulture till I felt I'd had enough. I grabbed a crabapple stick from near the dog box, then tromped into the field, swinging at the lying thing till it hissed in my face viciously and whooshed off.

Hard Knocks

Wrapped in a coat, by the roots of a tree,
with a marigold cap on his dusty-blond noggin
a shaken-up toddler no older than three

unzips his coat. By the roots of the tree
scattered the breadth of the snow-cloaked creek
lie the shattered remains of a scarlet toboggan.

Out of his coat, the boy leans on the tree
as the marigold sun lights the welt on his noggin.

Gein

*"'We discussed every murder we heard about. Eddie explained the
mistakes the murderer made.'"*

– Adeline Watkins, girlfriend (Life, Dec. 2, 1957)

Before the Terror of Plainfield
skinned dozens to fashion his lampshades,
his wastebaskets, seat covers and cereal bowls,
his window shades and bedposts—
not to mention the unspeakable
leggings, corset and mask—

a low horizon must have terrorized his heart.

For who can believe otherwise?
Who can believe one winter,
with the snow crests
hard and sharp as razors
over the barbwire
dividing the fields' mottled plots,
his child's eyes didn't scan
for the sear of sun
on summer grass?

If it were Christmas, 1913, who wouldn't understand?

If he liked to split his hands on barbwire?
Or if, once the last limp cow
had starved, been shot, he liked
to strip away his gloves and scarf
and stuff his forearms in the ice
till they went numb?

All that was left from his father's drinking
was the tanning shed out back, was his mother
warning, *Don't you trust no Smith's hooch,*
as she showed him how to skin a badger live
to make the hats they sold by Goult's
and he watched his dad's insurance flyers
dissolve into brown pulp
in the tannin vats.

All that was left, besides his mother
and brother, was the dog, Jeremiah,
soft, yellow pup,
only one to watch him
as he tottered through the knee-high drifts,
last gift his father got him
before they shut the grocery up
and the old man ran off.

And, anyhow, who wouldn't understand?

If on Christmas he cried over such
a big roast, if a full belly became a name
for love, and if it felt so soft and warm
pulling that yellow fur cap
over his wind-chapped ears?

My Old Man

What a fucking obstruction—
all fifty cubic feet of inlaid
oak, dingy with ink and cigarette
smoke, sitting square in my father's
longtime office, where his
soon-to-be-former secretary's stilettos
zipper like jackboots across
the low-pile carpet
and I, the only son around
to help him move.

In three months I'll come home to find him
planted on his couch, the upholstery full
of burn holes, him sucking on tin foil,
"getting the good cocaine out," the desk
clutter in some corner, scraped
and shattered, jetsam scattered
among the grandkids' toys.

But now my problem
is less the old man's retirement plans
than a matter of simple physics:

How the hell do we move this?

He just grunts, shifts his weight
off his bad hip, then shuffles out
the storefront while I stumble
over a run in the carpet,
thinking, *If I had a chainsaw
I'd tear the bastard in half.*

But of course I wouldn't
and don't. Instead, I check
if the desk's been cleared-out
and find the middle drawer still packed
with pens, sticky notes
and a half-filled legal pad—

When he still had it
together, he'd use
the glossy-green pen
with the gold finial
to mark up inventory, balance
his ledger, and sign his checks
with cavalier flourish.

And I picture him, freshly pressed
herringbone suit and all, diligently
scribbling a price on every yellow tag
that hung by a wire
around each sweepers' handle,
so that before I know it, I slip
the pen in my pocket, pull the drawer
from its runners, and tip the rest
in the trashcan.

By the time he waddles back with
the dolly, I've hefted the desk awry,
and he helps me slide it onto the toe plate.
Then, I dig my shoulder in and heave and strain

so that the broad, nicked-up desktop
shudders sideways,

and for the first time I see in full light
the kneehole where I used to hide,
when I was small enough
to carve my name on the inside
of the modesty.

The poem is

because, at five, I caught
my dad, his neck craned
in the dust-smothered,
olive-curtained, spare
room of our trailer,
scribbling and crying
on a near-exhausted legal pad
as my Uncle Don helped
shove his clothes in
a Rubbermaid bin.
Because, after dad left,
there was a warm divot
in my parents' comforter
where my brother and I
would lie like two blind puppies
stretched beneath a window,
before we'd lash our arms
around our mother
as she opened *Danny
the Dinosaur* to our
favorite page. Because
I first fell into myself
in second grade, the day
Mrs. Mann had us
write "poems" and when
my eyes turned to the playground
they suddenly divided
the sky from the rain. It is
because all this has recurred
in swells and waves:
The tear-soaked paper.
The empty bed. My son asking
for the peace *The Giving
Tree* gives. Now and then,
again and again—
when nothing's left,
the poem remains.

Lottery

My father never said anything
about what he'd have done
if he'd scratched off
a card to find
$ $ $
in a row.
Maybe he would've
just paid off the mortgage
or finished collecting those
restaurant matchbooks
he kept in a jar by
the glass-top stove.
Such mysteries though
must remain opaque. Even
Faustus says nothing
as the curtains close.

Elegy for My College Roommate

"'He might have severed my hands, my feet
and still yet would I weep
for fearless Fer Diad, tamer of steeds,
lies lifeless who was part of me.'"

– Táin Bó Cúalnge *(Cú Chulainn)*

1.

How surreal now we've become typical
              we used-to-be animals
                       all your old friends gathered in
your mother's darkened parlor
        now wearing blue paisley-print ties *for a bit of color*
                                     now
discussing the merits of L-tryptophan and child rearing
                over Styrofoam coffee cups—everything
white
   and spit-shined
        like the supporting cast
           of *Kramer vs. Kramer*—
                       everyone gabbing around
the only reason in ten years we've seen each other
           the once tight abs rocking black rags
                                   now
gusseted paunches.

But ain't it funny?
           I almost hear you say
           You all rallied to tattered standards now the shit's
hit?

Well listen, man,
        I never wanted to write this.

Because whatever *death* is
        it's not some non-sequitur splatter
                the cartoonish abra-cadaver
of the skeletons we'd skip Comm 105
        to watch Bruce Campbell hack into confetti. And *because*

whatever *death* is
>it's hardly as tidy as saying   *Videlicet: Life become as a sentence*
fragment. No,

all that presents itself
>even as the preacher turns
>>dismounts the pulpit
>>>>snaps his Bible shut
with no more wisdom to offer than a highway billboard
>are two essential
>>>>moth-eaten facts:
life is longer than you think
>and shorter than you know.

2.

The trivia of it is half what I recall, half
        what I must bite my lip
                and carry to my own plot of dirt:
knick-knacks
      a pair of black socks I've shuttled between ten dressers
                since junior year when we
packed our dorm—I tick off one more thing I owe you
          always meant to return
                    while memory
slips out like smoke.

What I know must have felt more crucial
        is now just two young assholes and two asshole-ettes
doing 90 down 76 through three states on election day
        naked
           flashing truckers
              jittery with coke
we swiped from the forensics lab—or just idiocy
        like the night you dried your nylon boxers in
our microwave
    turning them into napalm
        which we flung with a snapped curtain rod toward the
center of our quad
      where it burned a hole to the next story.

These aren't formative or whatever-our-shrinks-would-say—
                bullshit.
They're the missteps of young animals
      endowed with all life's brazen frenzy
          and as much sense
as a dime bag can offer.

Now, though, they also seem like strange justification
        a karmic scorecard of every instance
we should have died
    but didn't.

3.

Last time I saw you
                    I left you and your wife in a Southside motel
                                        with an Adderall and two
dozen cigarettes
                    buzzing in my veins like reverb
                                thinking, *How good for him, how good,*
as the sun pierced my eyes over Chicago's morning rush-hour
                                        and the sight that night of us
nodding out a head bang
                    while some teenager with a purple Mohawk
                                        whipped his lanky body
into the mosh pit
                    looped back through my mind and I thought
                                        with what this new me might call
fondness
            of all the times we sent our own manic limbs flailing.

But, at last glance, I wasn't a good friend.
                                All the old excuses
                                        "life getting in the way"
                                                        still ring
untrue—though I guess no one will blame me
                            least of all you
                                        since we all say what hurts each
other
        most.

And all that occurs is the literal tragedy
                    the hubris of thinking death will come on a May Day
float.
        Sure.
                What doesn't kill us
                            etc., etc.
                    But what does kill is usually ridiculous
                                        and petty and
small.

And all that comes to mind now is how our hearts
                        when their great gear-work finally corrodes
always conceal rusted springs
                    congenitally bad
                                actions.

And so we all wake as children
                to something we can't understand
                                and leave behind only barbaric
confusion
        a wildness that makes us
                jam our feet on the gas
                        turn our hood ornaments toward
the next nearest cliff
                and charge for an edge
                              that won't hold.

Tiny Rider

Death is a child.
You conceive her
when you first
hear her name.
At birth, she is
very small,
as are all things
seen far away.
She is so small
you're afraid
she might
blow out your
window. *I am on*
my way, she shouts
in a voice squeaky
as a mouse. You
wonder, What
will she look like
when she's close enough
to spot? Perhaps she will
seem stately, assured,
like your own
gray pate
when you go
of a heart attack
on New Year's Day
at eighty. Or maybe
romantic, sexy,
dramatic! A fiery halo
rising toward Heaven
so anonymous and tragic
she can't recognize
her own face. But
eventually, as she

gets so close
you can almost
make out
her tiny horse,
you decide not knowing
is part of the magic.
And besides, you think,
it's not like
if you guess right
you get a special pass.
Actually, you do,
she whispers.
Or, at least, you
might have, but now,
alas ... Then,
she sits with her
chin in her hands
and ponders what to do
without you.

What the Irish Sea Teaches

[At Sandycove, Ireland]

Let them break, your waves of words.
Let the tide collapse in rage.
Because there is a peace
in the ebb,
when the calls of herring gulls
can pacify a winter squall.
Give slake to the sea's woes
so later rising sound can fall
on ears like snapping cabbage palms,
like cracking beams in quaint beach homes,
like wind impacting storefront glass.
And then, and then, and then,
the sound will sound like this:

Dandelion

It's just
a weed
that doesn't
need
the flower it
makes
to reproduce.
Sure, you can
boil its leaves
and ferment
the juice
or make
a salad out
of its roots.
Living, though,
it has no use
except for maybe
to feed the bees.
It just ignores
all Darwin's rules
and shoves its
disheveled, yellow
head
up through
the fresh-cut
grass.

III

Coming In

Think you're escaping and run into yourself.
Longest way round is the shortest way home.

– *James Joyce,* Ulysses

A Poet Converses with His Muse

1.

I can say this life was something ecstatic
when I was a kid who only wanted to write books
lying naked on a bare mattress in a foreign city,
in an apartment without electricity,
buried in empty bottles and cigarette butts,
listening as an equally vibrant she
serenaded our wasting youths at sunrise.
It was a moment when we still felt
we could be everything, a youthful singularity
where flying pink elephants played croquet
with purple dragons across the rafters.
Now, everyone else has left the party
and I'm still playing the same cracked tune
in a mess of yesterday's confetti.
If I had a green light to go toward
it might be worth getting myself shot for,
but even that has vanished
as I float into a vast Atlantic current
of mixed metaphors and depressiveness.
But if I could just believe again
that anyone cared beyond reason
I might feel that gasp of new breath,
like the morning air my first days in Amsterdam,
St. Petersburg, Dublin, Berlin ...
when even the garbage seemed
pleasantly fragrant. Instead,
I'm just stumbling into a comfy dotage
of lap blankets, tea, and murder mysteries
with what feels like an anvil on my chest.
And there isn't even a wily old lady to hold my hand
because I pissed away every ounce of human affection,
chasing this thing called *writing*, which I now know
is nothing but pain.

2.

Poet, forgive such a measured reply—
it's not to sound scornful, sarcastic or curt
but merely my manner in matters like this,
for tact is a tactic that's rarely awry—
but first, to your point about feeling ignored
you know how my Emily shared in such woes.
And then there was Whitman, well-known yet despised:
he hardly achieved the acceptance he sought.
You see, it's not me who grants wealth or renown;
mine is the business of image and song,
of which, as a favorite, you've had quite a lot,
so why cast your eyes after what you're without?
And I'm no Apollo or Bacchus, you'll find—
in fact, some would argue I'm born from your thoughts.
So please be contented with what I can offer,
the symbols and music you started to pray for
back when I gazed through a window at you,
a child whose father was neck-deep in drink,
and watching your Christmas tree fall in the fray,
you scratched out a poem in love with the path
the snowflakes traced tumbling down through the air
and learned you'd forgotten for moments your pain.
My method was simple then, plain and sincere:
I whispered some verses with which you'd connect,
and Clement Moore's rhythm and light-hearted rhymes
put presents and sugar-plums back in your head.
Suppose what *you* write is some other kid's savior:
who then could call it a senseless endeavor?
For that's why I've helped you and why I remain
despite all the critical things you now say.

Hours

To St. Pius,
defender from too many cigarettes,
let me not smoke the lucky too soon
nor let me set
off the fire alarm
in any airport restrooms
nor let the butts
in my overfull ashtrays
fall to the floor smoldering
beside my particleboard bookshelf.
Please note: especially remember
this final favor
when I am reading
on the toilet.

†

To St. Raphael,
succor for the good sex,
let not my left nut
know what my right is doing.
Preserve me from the stranger
but also from brown mystery growths.
And lead me not into titty bars
with girls whose hand jobs
give patrons a Brazilian
contact STD
that makes a guy's dick shed
like a garter snake.

†

To St. Thomas More,
fiery sword of divorce attorneys,
sow nothing less than chain lightning
in my lawyer's eyes. Transform her
into Kali, Boudicca and Xena,
Joan of Arc and Pallas Athena,
all infused in one tangerine pantsuit.
Let her tongue spit venomous
dropkicks before the bench.
Let her words erupt

with an atomic Kung-Fu grip.
Let her protect me
like my own mother.

✝

To St. Rita,
sister to the lonesome,
let not my despondency over her
who once shot through my breath,
once made me believe
I would drown as our hands
grazed, consume me
in the rituals of heartbreak;
remember me to mornings
and the sweetness of sunlight
through the curtains of my tiny studio
even when she is no longer
warmed beside me.

✝

To St. Felicitas,
patron of the small and lost,
let me still be the vanquisher
of burnt-out nightlights
and slayer of gray reflections
he spies in closets, under beds
and down dark hallways
until, someday, I am that grizzled face
whose hand he squeezes
as he huddles over
the paper-white sheets
where my breath
shudders and breaks.

Epigram for My Son on His Third Birthday

Small fry, little guy,
cutest in the world,
he plays guitar and drives a car
and flirts with all the girls.

Given the Day

Mornings I am given the day,

given the day, with all its tallow light squeezing my eyelids like a
tightening blindfold,

given the day with a soft grind in the back of my skull, the starter of my
synapses spitting and misfiring,

given the day as I open my eyes to the hanging arabesques of last night's
smoke,

given the day in a half-forgotten litany of responsibilities that stray like
feral cats inside my brainpan—

given the crinkled electric bill, the dishes coated with grot in my sink,
rent due, emails from clients asking to reschedule, the bloated,
made-up faces of the anchors and pundits and politicians on the
morning news, I am still

given the day, given the keen bite of coffee slaloming through the sluice
of my teeth,

given the stacks of unread books I have given up cramming into my
bookshelf so their covers trap my gaze with soft-toned blues and
greens,

given the words to be strung then nailed in place, then replaced gently
like cogs in a watch housing,

given the mousy barista with the lavender perfume who rings up my
lunch each day,

given the wherewithal to eat three squares after years of homelessness
and starvation and living in a hotel room where the toilets never
flushed and the shower never drained,

and given the bister and vermillion plait of corn and soy on two-lane
Illinois roads,

I am given the way my son's eyes widen into quiet smiles as my ex opens
the door,

given the way she smiles too, as if in just that instant, we could forget all
we can't undo and the noose of history that dangles from our necks.

(But, given love and giving love, what can't a heart forget?)

Given the smell of new toys, of popcorn and a box of peanut M&Ms
freshly opened in a dark theater's cozy void

given my new perspective on campy action sequences, the CGI shrapnel
hurling at me with cartoonish booms as my son sits rapt in
wonderment,

and, given all this, what haven't I been given?

Even as my son is given over to sleep,

even as he is, in turn, given back into the arms of a woman I gave more
than I thought I had,

even as I slide between the comforter and sheet of my twin-size and
switch on Forensic Files for sleep,

given this day and so many like it, when the calm in my chest is such
that I give no thought to being bored—for all these things,

for being given the day, I give thanks to each day

if only to be given more.

How to Be the Best Dad Ever

Remember yourself.
Sit on the floor in new clothes
and learn to smash tin
cars against the wall, shoot squirt
guns at the cat, be at peace.

Of Beauty & Things

These things need saving:

the bleary carnival lights
streaked across a Saturday night
sky, the schmutz on vinyl siding
on dingy, little
intersection homes, the filmy air sliding
between the eye and an American flag
or church when these things
are not seen
on postcards or screens.

The taste of too much
grease on your tongue
after eating funnel cake and deep-fried
Oreos both, and the smooth, tanned legs
the girls-you-know show
from cut-offs
with their inside pockets dangling loose
beneath the fringe.

The rattle of rust-rotted shocks
when the kids peel out of Taco Bell
and the glow always over
the cornfields, always some
orgiastic rattle on the breeze.

Please, God, if all this must go,
sure, let us save all the perfect things,
all the As Seen On TV things,
but also may we save
a few small, imperfect things,
some actual breath
from actual throats?

Let me, for instance, save
the smell of gasoline
and of musty pissed-on clothes
at a laundromat without air or heat,

save a single pillar
of factory smoke, a stray tin can
from the garbage along the road,
and just a smidge
of that brackish, mushy shit
that lays on fresh-plowed snow.

Save how my father inflates his upper lip
when thinking, how my mother's
weak chin and hooked nose
make her look like a goose,
and how my brother's crow's feet cinch
like drawstring bags
when he is about to tell
a dirty joke.

But, above all, save
my baby's puffy cheeks,
how he laughs
with both eyes closed.

Valediction

As the long minutes furrow
our eyelids and mouths, we
start to fear what we can't believe.
We plant our heels
ever deeper in dirt
and learn to love
our own chipped teeth.

Call it barbaric, medieval,
you can't forget being yanked
from a folding steel chair
at three and spanked
bare-assed in front of
your church. And between
the plush flesh of inner thighs
and Heaven's gilt chateau,
where brass lamps all dissolve
into *wisdom* and *cold*
is always pretending to be snow,
we all borrow
against our souls.

So try a bite of caviar, escargot,
note the semen-like scent
of cherry blossoms
and the cashmere cardigan of your first
kiss, hear *Ode to Joy* crescendo
as specks of cobalt and crimson split
the Fourth of July gloam—

                              not as a thief
fondles a necklace, or a collector sleeves
a coin, but as a sinner
receives communion, bent and bowed
at the grace in forgetting all
she can't un-know.

Acknowledgements

I would like to thank the editors of the following magazines and journals in which these poems have appeared or will appear, often in radically different forms and occasionally under different titles:

Arsenic Lobster: "Hard to Say" – *Cha: An Asian Literary Journal:* "St. Petersburg Has Many Churches"; "What I Said to Her Was Not a Lie" – *The Axe Factory Review:* "When the last one left" as "Where I Draw the Line" – *Broad River Review:* "Of Beauty & Things" (2018); "Triangle" (2019) – *The Cimarron Review:* "A Poet Converses with His Muse" – *The Crab Creek Review:* "The Stenographers Union" – *Danse Macabre:* "St. Petersburg Has Many Churches" (Reprint) – *decomP:* "Dandelion" – *Heartbreaker Magazine:* "Counter-play" – *The Heartland Review:* "Valediction" as "Valediction on Zero: A Postscript" – *the idiom:* "Between You and Me" as "This Statement is False" – *Kind Writers:* "Gein" – *Molotov Cocktail:* "Why the Coyote Doesn't Just Order Chinese" – *Inlandia:* "Chicago Tableau" (Reprint) – *Noctua:* "Woman Hips, Woman Lips, Woman Spine" – *Orbis:* "Outside Odessa" – *The Literary Hatchet:* "Chicago Tableau" – *Poetry Journal in Print:* "Too Funny"; "Woman Hips, Woman Lips, Woman Spine" (Reprint); "The poem is" (Reprint) – *Rats Ass Review:* "Poet as the Sea"; "Snapchat Triolet"; "Hard Knocks" – *Sheila-Na-Gig:* "My Old Man"; "Hours"; "Given the Day" – *Sons & Daughters:* "Epigram for the Neanderthals"; "How It Goes" – *Third Wednesday:* "Gen Y Love Poem" as "Gen Y Love Poem I" – *Vine Leaves Journal:* "Now"; "The poem is" – *Voice & Verse:* "St. Petersburg Has Many Churches" (Reprint) – *Word Riot:* "Lottery"

Additionally, the poems "When the last one left," "A New Kind of Vegan," "Los Dos Joaquines," "Lottery," "What I Said to Her Was Not a Lie," "Between You and Me," "Counter-play," "Outside Odessa," "St. Petersburg Has Many Churches," "Hard to Say" and "Dandelion" previously appeared in the chapbook *The Day the Sun Rolled Out of the Sky*, printed in three editions by Cy Gist Press (2010-2013), while "The fattest monk in history" was also published by Cy Gist as a limited-edition broadside in two editions (2013); "Hard to Say," "Between You and Me" and "Why the Coyote Doesn't Just Order Chinese" were collected in the anthologies *Arsenic Lobster 2011 Anthology, The Idiom Magazine: Anthology of Volumes 1 & 2* and *The Molotov Cocktail: Prize Winners Anthology Vol. 3,* respectively; "Gen Y Love Poem" was reprinted by The Atrocious Poets both in their chapbook anthology *Cut Poems from Air: Poetry Honoring Gwendolyn Brooks* and as a limited-edition broadside after initially appearing in a slightly different form in *Third Wednesday*; and "Too Funny," "Woman Hips, Woman Lips, Woman Spine" and "The poem is" appeared alongside translations into Vietnamese by Khe Iem in several issues of *Poetry Journal in Print*. As for the translated epigraphs appearing herein, all, including those from Middle English, Middle Irish, Medieval Tuscan Italian, Old Norse Icelandic, Modern High German and Langue d'Oïl Old French, are my own and original to the present work.

Further, "My Old Man," "Hours" and "Given the Day" were jointly awarded Sheila-Na-Gig's Fall 2017 Quarterly Prize; "Triangle" was short-listed for the Fourth Eyewear Fortnight Prize and was subsequently selected as a finalist for the *Broad River Review's* 2018 Rash Award by Maurice Manning; "Gen Y Love Poem" was selected as a finalist for the Writing Salon's 2018 Jane Underwood Prize by Arisa White and as a finalist for the Atrocious Poets' Gwendolyn Brooks Prize by Mojdeh Stoakley and Donald G. Evans; "The Stenographers Union" was named a finalist for the 2017 *Crab Creek Review* Prize by Diane Seuss; "Of Beauty & Things" was named an Honorable Mention Finalist for the *Broad River Review's* 2017 Rash Award by Bill Brown; "Why the Coyote Doesn't Just Order Chinese" was awarded eighth place in Molotov Cocktail's 2017 Shadow Award; "St. Petersburg Has Many Churches" received nominations from *Asian Cha* for the Best of the Net and Pushcart prizes; and "Given the Day" received a Best of the Net nomination from *Sheila-Na-Gig*.

Major thanks are due as well to the Poets & Writers and PEN America organizations and the Authors League Fund for their generosity in selecting me as a grant recipient during the 2020 COVID-19 crisis; without all three organizations' immense kindness, shepherding the present collection from manuscript to book form would have been a far more onerous undertaking in difficult times.

Finally, special thanks are due to the many friends and mentors who have offered encouragement and, at times, patiently helped me hone this collection and the various poems in it over the past fifteen years, including (in no particular order) Marvin Bell, Zachary Schomburg, Tammy Ho Lai-Ming, Allison Eir Jenks, R.S. Gwynn, Shirley Geok-lin Lim, Josh Williams, Anna Marie Wheeler, Mark Lamoureux, Alfred Corn, David Kirby, Erin Belieu, Mark Weiss, Joe Farley, Chris Hosea and Joe Weil, as well as Drs. Larry Grimes and Walton Turner, who encouraged my early poetry and offered invaluable formative reading suggestions while I was a student at Bethany College, and my graduate advisors and readers at WV Wesleyan, Doug Van Gundy, Mary Carroll-Hackett, Jessie van Eerden, Richard Schmitt, Mark DeFoe, Rebecca Gayle Howell and Devon McNamara. But, most of all, I owe a debt of gratitude to my parents and son for showing me the love that inspired this collection and the patience and support that allowed me to see it to fruition.

Vine Leaves Press

Enjoyed this book?
Go to *vineleavespress.com* to find more.

CPSIA information can be obtained
at www.ICGtesting.com
Printed in the USA
FSHW011812131120
75741FS